SPORTY JOKES

Scholastic Children's Books
Euston House, 24 Eversholt Street
London NW1 1DB

A division of Scholastic Ltd
London ~ New York ~ Toronto ~ Sydney ~ Auckland
Mexico City ~ New Delhi ~ Hong Kong

First published in the UK by Scholastic Ltd, 2016

Text by Toby Reynolds
Illustrations by Andrew Pinder

© Scholastic Children's Books, 2016

ISBN 978 1407 16210 2

Printed and bound by CPI Group (UK) Ltd, Croydon, CR0 4YY

2 4 6 8 10 9 7 5 3 1

Gigglers

SPORTY JOKES

Toby Reynolds

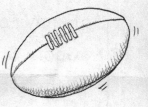

Illustrated by
Andrew Pinder

■ SCHOLASTIC

Contents

Absurd
Athletics

Q. What is harder to catch the faster you run?
A. Your breath!

Q. Why do marathon runners make good students?
A. Because education pays off in the long run!

Q. What is a runner's favourite subject in school?
A. Jog-raphy!

Q. What happened to the world's worst athlete?
A. He ran a bath and came in second!

Q. What do athletes do when they're not running?
A. Surf the sprinternet!

Q. Why don't sprinters listen to music?
A. Because they are always breaking their own records!

Q. Why did the athlete refuse to do the long jump?
A. Because he was short-sighted!

Q. What happened when the two waves had a race?
A. They tide!

Q. Who was the fastest runner of all time?
A. Adam. He was first in the human race!

Q. Why were all the hurdle events cancelled?
A. It wasn't a leap year!

Q. Why did the sprinter bring his barber to the track?
A. Because he wanted to shave a few seconds off his time!

Q. Why did the bald man take up running?
A. He wanted to get some fresh 'air!

Q. What are the two things that could stop you becoming the best athlete in the world?
A. Your feet!

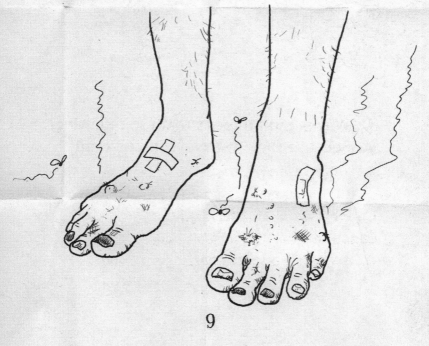

Q. How do you start a jelly race?
A. Get set!

Q. How do you start a firefly race?
A. Ready, steady, glow!

Q. Why is the athletics team so revolting?
A. Because they're always discus-ting!

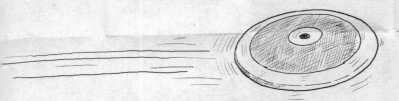

Q. What do you become if you run behind a car?
A. Exhausted!

Q. Did you hear about the marathon runner who ran for three hours but only moved two feet?
A. He only had two feet!

Q. How do you start a teddy bear race?
A. Ready, teddy, go!

Q. What's a banker's favourite Olympic event?
A. Vault!

Q. Who is the most handsome athlete?
A. The sprinter, because he's always dashing!

A woman meets a man carrying a two and a half metre-long metal stick and asks, "Are you a pole vaulter?"
"No," says the man, "I'm German. But how did you know my name is Walter?"

Q. Two silk worms were in a race. Who won?
A. It was a tie!

Q. What happened to the marathon runner whose shoes were too small?
A. She suffered the agony of defeat!

Q. What happened when a tap, a lettuce and a tomato had a race?
A. The tap was running, the lettuce was a head and the tomato couldn't ketchup!

Archery Antics

Q. What kind of bow can't be tied?
A. A crossbow!

Q. What is it called when two archers score the same?
A. A bowtie!

Q. Why did the arrow-maker get sacked?
A. He was missing the point!

Q. What did the archer say when she nearly got shot at an archery contest?
A. Wow, that was an arrow escape!

Q. Did you hear about the archer who shot an arrow into the air?
A. He missed!

Q. What did the archer get when he hit a bullseye?
A. A very angry bull!

Q. How does an archer tie his shoelaces?
A. With a long bow!

Q. What do you get when you cross an archer with a gift-wrapper?
A. Ribbon Hood!

Q. Why did the man find archery too frustrating?
A. Because it has so many drawbacks!

Badminton Buffoonery

Q. What is Count Dracula's favourite sport?
A. Bat-minton!

Q. What did the shuttlecock say when it got hit?
A. Who's making all that racquet?

Q. What's a sheep's favourite game?
A. Baa-dminton!

Tom: Why did the badminton player go to prison?
Tim: Because he was a bad man, Tom!

Q. What do you call a bald man in a wedding dress?
A. A shuttlecock!

Q. How do hens encourage their favourite badminton players?
A. They egg them on!

Barmy Basketball

Q. Why are basketball players messy eaters?
A. They're always dribbling!

Q. What do you get if you cross a basketball with a newborn snake?
A. A bouncing baby boa!

Q. Why can't you play basketball with pigs?
A. They always hog the ball!

Q. Why was Cinderella such a bad basketball player?
A. Her coach was a pumpkin!

Q. What do you call an unbelievable story about a basketball player?
A. A tall tale!

Q. What's the difference between a dog and a basketball player?
A. One drools and the other dribbles!

Q. What do you do when you see an elephant with a basketball?
A. Get out of the way!

20

Q. Why was the kangaroo invited to join the basketball team?
A. He was good at jump shots!

Q. Why did the basketball player go to jail?
A. Because he shot the ball!

Q. Why do basketball players love doughnuts?
A. Because they can dunk them!

Q. Why did the chicken cross the basketball court?
A. Because the referee called foul!

Q. How do you play basketball in Hawaii?
A. With hula-hoops!

1st sports fan: I hear they are feeding the basketball players bananas before each game.
2nd sports fan: Does it make them shoot any better?
1st sports fan: No. But it makes the game more a-peel-ing!

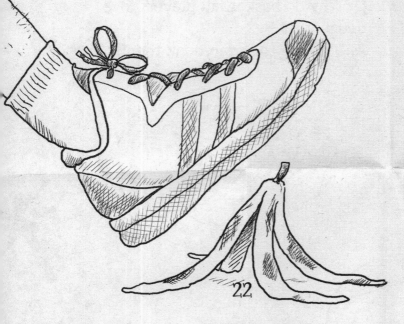

1st basketball player: We're going to win this game – don't you think?
2nd basketball player: I certainly hoop so!

Q. Why did the old basketball player become a judge?
A. He wanted to stay on the court!

Q. Why were the chicken, turkey, pheasant and goose allowed on the basketball court, but not the duck?
A. Because at a basketball game, five fouls and you're out!

Boisterous Boxing

Q. When do boxers start wearing gloves?
A. When it gets cold!

Q. What ring is square?
A. A boxing ring!

Q. How did the featherweight boxer win all his fights?
A. He tickled his opponents!

24

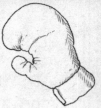

Q. What is the best part of a boxer's joke?
A. The punch line!

Q. How do you make a fruit punch?
A. Give it boxing lessons!

Q. What does a boxer ask for at the hairdresser?
A. An uppercut!

Q. What is the difference between a boxer and a man with a cold?
A. One knows his blows and the other blows his nose!

Q. What do you call a boxer who gets beaten up in a fight?
A. A sore loser!

Q. What's the difference between a nail and a boxer?
A. One's knocked in and the other's knocked out!

Q. Does a match box?
A. No, but a tin can!

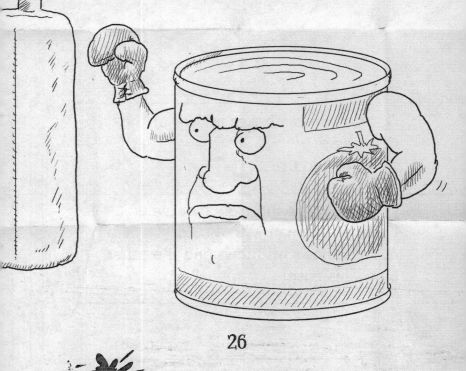

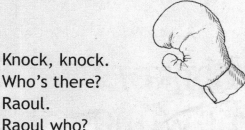

Knock, knock.
Who's there?
Raoul.
Raoul who?
Raoul with the punches!

Q. What happened when Santa took up boxing?
A. He decked the halls!

Q. Why did the boxer wear gloves to bed?
A. Because he wanted to hit the sack!

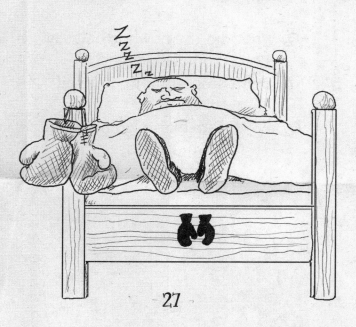

27

Bonkers Bowling

Q. What is the world's quietest sport?
A. Bowling, because you can hear a pin drop!

Q. What did the bowling ball say to the bowling pins?
A. Don't stop me, I'm on a roll!

Q. Which cats like to go bowling?
A. Alley cats!

Bowler 1: I was asked to leave the bowling team after I knocked all the pins down in one go.
Bowler 2: That doesn't seem fair!
Bowler 1: The pins were in the next alley!

Q. What should you do with old bowling balls?
A. Give them to elephants to use as marbles!

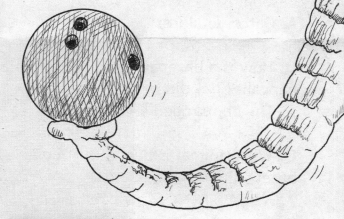

Q. What happened to the girl who took her knitting to the bowling alley?
A. She got pins and needles!

Brilliant
Baseball

Q. What did the baseball glove say to the baseball?
A. Catch you later!

Q. How is a baseball team similar to a pancake?
A. They both need a good batter!

Q. What animal is best at hitting a baseball?
A. A bat!

Q. How do baseball players stay cool?
A. They sit next to the fans!

Q. Why are baseball players so rich?
A. Because they play on diamonds!

Q. Why are criminals great baseball players?
A. Because they already know how to hit, run and steal!

Q. What goes all the way around a baseball field but never moves?
A. The fence!

Comic Cricket

Q. When is cricket a crime?
A. When there's a hit and run!

Q. Why can't Robin play cricket?
A. Because he's lost his bat, man!

Q. How do you stop moles digging up the cricket pitch?
A. Hide their spades!

Q. Why was the Egyptian mummy no good at cricket?
A. Because he was too wrapped up in himself!

Q. What did the cricket pitch say to the player?
A. I hate it when people treat me like dirt!

Q. Why did the vampires cancel the cricket game?
A. Because they couldn't find their bats!

Knock, knock.
Who's there!
Cricket.
Cricket who?
Cricket neck means I can't lift anything!

Q. What do you get when you cross a bowler with a carpet?
A. A throw rug!

Q. Which team play cricket in their underwear?
A. The Vest Indies!

Q. What is an insect's favourite sport?
A. Cricket!

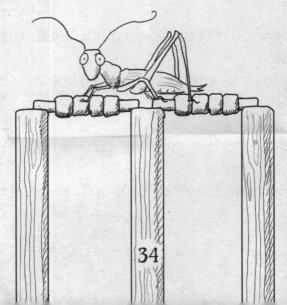

Cycling Capers

Q. Why couldn't the bicycle stand up?
A. Because it was two tyred!

Knock, knock.
Who's there?
Isabelle.
Isabelle who?
Isabelle necessary on a bicycle?

Q. What's the hardest part of learning to ride a bike?
A. The pavement!

Q. What do you get if you cross a bike and a flower?
A. Bicycle petals!

Q. What do you call a bicycle built by a chemist?
A. Bike-carbonate of soda!

Q. When is a bicycle not a bicycle?
A. When it turns into a driveway!

Q. Why don't bankers make good cyclists?
A. They tend to lose their balance!

Q. What does a racing bike call its dad?
A. Pop-cycle!

Q. How do crazy cyclists travel through the forest?
A. They take the psycho path!

Q. What's big, scary and has three wheels?
A. A monster riding a tricycle!

Q. Why did the little boy take his bicycle to bed with him?
A. Because he didn't want to walk in his sleep!

Q. What is a ghost-proof bicycle?
A. One with no spooks in it!

Q. What do you call an artist who sculpts with bicycle parts?
A. Cycleangelo!

Funny Football

Q. What do you call it when T-Rex scores a goal?
A. A dino-score!

Q. How did the football pitch end up as triangle?
A. Somebody took a corner!

Q. What is a ghost's favourite position in football?
A. Ghoul keeper!

Q. What do footballers and magicians have in common?
A. They both do hat tricks!

Q. Which goalkeeper can jump higher than a crossbar?
A. All of them, a crossbar can't jump!

Q. What did the footballer say to the football?
A. I get a kick out of you!

Q. Why do artists never win at football?
A. Because they keep drawing!

Q. What type of football players do bank managers like the most?
A. Goalkeepers, because they are the best savers!

Q. What is a footballer's favourite drink?
A. Penal-tea!

Q. Where do footballers go to dance?
A. The foot-ball!

Q. What did the left football boot say to the right football boot?
A. Between us we should have a ball!

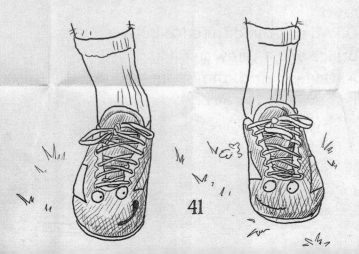

Q. What did the bumblebee striker say?
A. Hive scored!

Q. Which insect is useless in goal?
A. A fumble bee!

Q. When is a football player like a grandfather clock?
A. When he is a striker!

Q. What is the difference between a prince and a throw-in?
A. One is heir to the throne and the other is thrown to the air!

CHANGING ROOM

Q. What part of a football pitch
smells nicest?
A. The scenter spot!

Q. What did the footballer say when
he accidentally burped during
a game?
A. Sorry, it was a freak hic!

Q. What part of a football stadium
never stays the same?
A. The changing rooms!

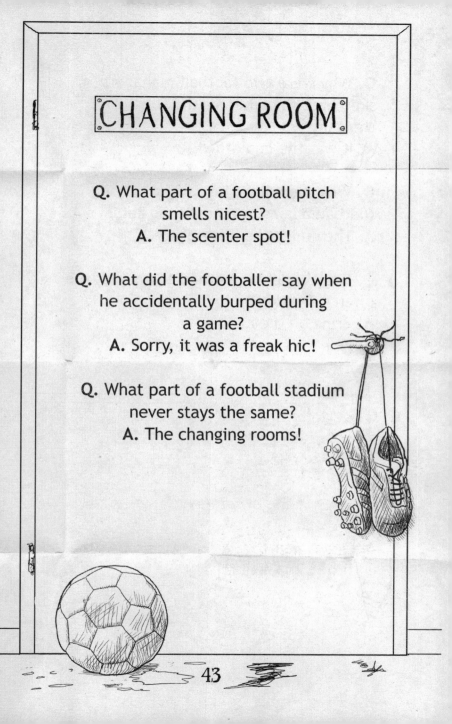

43

Q. Why were two football managers sketching china before the start of the game?
A. It was the cup draw!

Q. Why should you be careful playing football against a team of big cats?
A. They might be cheetahs!

Q. What should a football team do if the pitch is flooded?
A. Bring on their subs!

Q. What do you call a girl who stands inside goalposts and stops the ball rolling away?
A. Annette!

Q. What ship holds 20 football teams but only three leave it each season?
A. The Premier-ship!

Q. Which football side did Shy Barry and Very Quiet Vernon play for?
A. The reserve-d team!

Q. Why did the football quit the team?
A. It was tired of being kicked around!

Q. What spins around and around and chants 'Here we go, here we go, here we go!'
A. A football fan!

Q. Why were football fans once like old cars?
A. They never went anywhere without a rattle!

Q. What is a snake's favourite football team?
A. Slitherpool!

Q. What is pink, has four legs and plays football?
A. Queens Pork Rangers!

Q. What do you call a football team crossed with ice cream?
A. Aston Vanilla!

Q. What do earwigs sing at football matches?
A. 'Earwig-o, Earwig-o, Earwig-o!'

Q. What is a striker's favourite song?
A. Shake, rattle and goal!

Q. Why is Dracula a hopeless goalkeeper?
A. He hates crosses!

Q. What is a goalkeeper's favourite lunch?
A. Beans on post!

Q. Why do ghosts go to football matches?
A. So they can boo the referee!

Q. Why did the goalpost get angry?
A. Because the bar was rattled!

Q. What runs along the edge of the pitch but never moves?
A. The sideline!

Q. What has 22 legs and two wings but can't fly?
A. A football team!

Goofy Golf

Q. Why did the golfer have an extra pair of trousers?
A. In case he got a hole in one!

Q. Why did Tarzan spend so much time on the golf course?
A. He was perfecting his swing!

Q. Why type of top should you wear while golfing?
A. A tee-shirt!

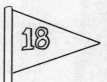

Q. What's a golfer's favourite letter?
A. Tee!

Q. When is the best time to play golf?
A. Tee-time!

Q. What goes putt-putt-putt-putt-putt-putt?
A. A really bad golfer!

Golfer: Do you think my game is improving?
Caddy: Yes, sir. You miss the ball much closer now.

Q. Where did the rock star go to play golf?
A. Pebble beach!

Q. How many golfers does it take to change a light bulb?
A. Fore!

Golfer: This is the worst course I've ever played on.
Caddy: This isn't the golf course. We left that an hour ago.

Golfer: Do you like my game?
Caddy: Very good, sir! But personally I prefer golf.

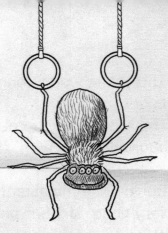

Gymnastics Gags

Q. What do bananas do best in gymnastics?
A. The splits!

Q. What did the Egyptian mummy coach say at the end of gymnastics practice?
A. Let's wrap this up!

Q. Why shouldn't you pick on a gymnast?
A. You never know when they might flip!

Q. Why did the gymnasts get married?
A. Because they were head over heels in love!

Q. Why do gymnasts make great friends?
A. They'll always do you a good turn and will bend over backwards to help!

Q. Why was the gymnast waving her bank statements in the air?
A. She wanted to display her great balance!

Hilarious Horse Racing

Q. What's a racehorse's favourite
TV show?
A. Neighbours!

Q. Which side of a racehorse has more
hair?
A. The outside!

A racehorse owner takes his sick horse
to the vet. "Will I be able to race him
again?" he asks.
The vet replies, "Yes! And you'll probably
win!"

Q. Why should you never be rude to a jump jockey?
A. In case he takes offence (a fence)!

Q. Did you hear about the racehorse that got a job in a watch factory?
A. All he did was stand around making faces!

Q. What happened when the racehorse ran with an apple in his mouth?
A. He was pipped at the post!

Q. What do racehorses like to eat?
A. Fast food!

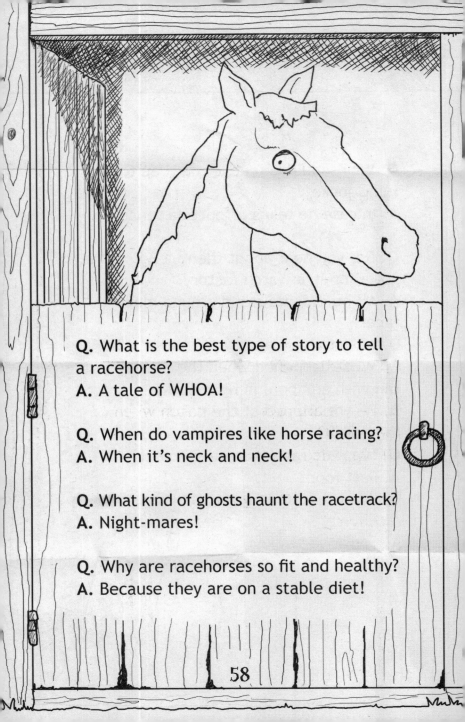

Q. What is the best type of story to tell a racehorse?
A. A tale of WHOA!

Q. When do vampires like horse racing?
A. When it's neck and neck!

Q. What kind of ghosts haunt the racetrack?
A. Night-mares!

Q. Why are racehorses so fit and healthy?
A. Because they are on a stable diet!

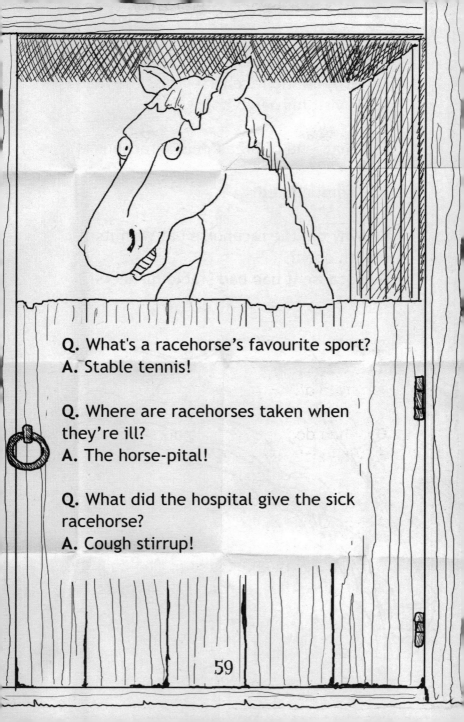

Q. What's a racehorse's favourite sport?
A. Stable tennis!

Q. Where are racehorses taken when they're ill?
A. The horse-pital!

Q. What did the hospital give the sick racehorse?
A. Cough stirrup!

Q. Why did the racehorse cross the road?
A. To visit his *neigh*-bour!

Q. What kind of bread does a racehorse eat?
A. Thoroughbred!

Q. Why did the racehorse eat with its mouth open?
A. Because it had bad stable manners!

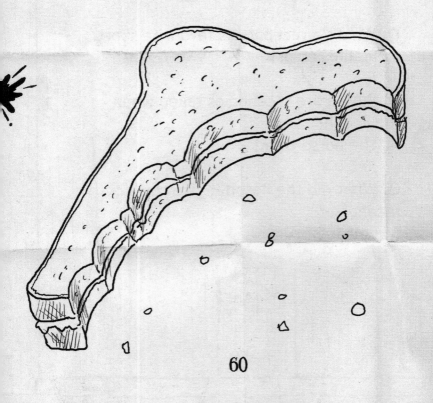

Q. How do you know when a racehorse is really slow?
A. The jockey keeps a diary of his trip around the racecourse!

Q. Why did the jockey stand behind the horse?
A. He thought he might get a kick out of it!

Q. What is the difference between a racehorse and a duck?
A. One goes quick and the other goes quack!

Q. What did the horse say when he fell over?
A. I can't giddy-up!

Q. What do you say to an impatient jockey?
A. Hold your horses!

Q. What is the difference between a racehorse and the weather?
A. One is reined up, the other rains down!

Hysterical Hockey

Q. What helps ghosts to win hockey matches?
A. Their team spirit!

Q. Why couldn't the car play hockey?
A. Because it only had one boot!

Q. Why couldn't the pig play hockey?
A. Because he had pulled his hamstring!

Q. Why did the chicken get sent off?
A. For persistent fowl play!

Q. What happens if it rains and rains and the hockey pitch is knee-deep in water?
A. They turn on the floodlights!

Q. What did the hockey coach say to the player who lost the ball?
A. Find it quickly or I'll give you some stick!

Q. Did you hear about the two flies playing hockey in a saucer?
A. They were practising for the cup!

Q. How do you stop squirrels playing hockey in the garden?
A. Hide the ball – it drives them nuts!

Incredible Ice Skating

Q. What did the ice skater say to the ice when she slipped?
A. I'm gonna let it slide this time!

Q. How is music like ice skating?
A. If you don't 'C sharp' you'll 'B flat'!

Q. How long does it take to learn to ice skate?
A. A few sittings!

Q. Why is it dangerous to tell a joke while ice skating?
A. Because the ice might crack up!

Martial Arts Madness

Q. Which martial art do vegetarians study?
A. Kung-Tofu!

Q. Why don't karate experts salute?
A. They might hurt their heads!

Q. Why didn't the skeleton go to judo?
A. He had no body to go with!

Q. Why is the skeleton afraid to do karate?
A. Because he doesn't have any guts!

Q. What do Chinese wrestlers have for breakfast?
A. Kung food!

Q. Did you hear about the new karate video?
A. It became a hit and a blockbuster!

Q. Why did the karate expert wear a black belt?
A. To keep his trousers up!

Q. What do you call a pig that does karate?
A. A pork chop!

Ridiculous Rugby

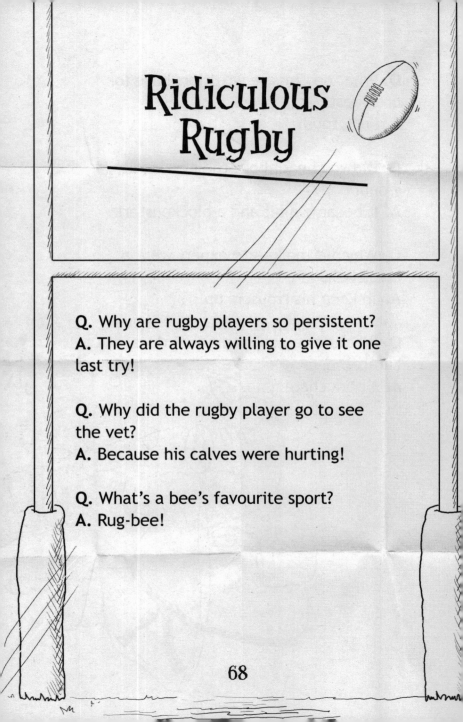

Q. Why are rugby players so persistent?
A. They are always willing to give it one last try!

Q. Why did the rugby player go to see the vet?
A. Because his calves were hurting!

Q. What's a bee's favourite sport?
A. Rug-bee!

Q. Why aren't rugby stadiums built in outer space?
A. Because there is no atmosphere!

Q. What trees can't you climb at a rugby ground?
A. The lavatories!

A rugby player went to the doctor: "When I got back from the game I found that when I touched my legs, my arms, my head, my tummy and everywhere else, it really hurt".
The doctor said: "You've broken your finger".

Q. What lights up a rugby stadium?
A. A rugby match!

Side-Splitting Swimming

Q. Why did the man keep doing backstroke?
A. Because he had just eaten and didn't want to swim on a full stomach!

Q. Why can't two elephants go swimming together?
A. Because they only have one pair of trunks between them!

Q. When is your swimming costume like a bell?
A. When you wring it out!

Q. How can you swim a mile in just a few seconds?
A. Swim over a waterfall!

Q. Where do zombies go swimming?
A. The Dead Sea!

Q. Where do ghosts like to go swimming?
A. Lake Eerie!

Q. What kind of swimming stroke can you use on toast?
A. BUTTER-fly!

Q. What is a polar bear's favourite stroke?
A. Blubber-fly!

Q. How do people swimming in the ocean say hi to each other?
A. They wave!

Q. In which direction does a chicken swim?
A. Cluck-wise!

Q. What word looks the same backwards and upside down?
A. SWIMS

Q. Which kind of exercises are best for a swimmer?
A. Pool-ups!

Q. What stroke do sheep enjoy doing?
A. The *baaaa*ckstroke!

Silly Sailing

Q. What is a sailor's favourite snack?
A. Chocolate ship cookies!

Q. Why do sailors always carry bags of dried fruit?
A. In case they get into trouble, the currants could carry them ashore!

Q. What day is the best to go sailing?
A. Winds-day!

Q. Why can't you build a fire in a kayak?
A. You can't have your kayak and heat it!

Knock, knock.
Who's there?
Canoe.
Canoe who?
Canoe come out and play?

Q. Why did the boy take his skipping rope onto the ship?
A. He wanted to become the skipper!

Q. What happens when sailing boats get really old?
A. They keel over!

Q. What do sailors put on their soup?
A. Crew-tons!

Q. Why did the captain lose the yacht race?
A. He found himself in a no-wind situation!

Q. How do retired sailors greet each other?
A. Long time, no sea!

Q. How does a boat show affection?
A. It hugs the shore!

Q. How do sailors get their clothes clean?
A. They throw them overboard and they wash ashore!

Spectacular Sports Day

Q. Why don't eggs enjoy the egg-and-spoon race?
A. They can't take a yolk!

Q. Did you hear about the two men who ran in the fathers' race at sports day?
A. One ran in short bursts, the other in burst shorts!

Q. What happened to the boy with a fear of hurdles?
A. He got over it!

Q. Why did the school's best athlete lose the decathlon?
A. She had a slipped discus!

Q. Why did the boy come first in the 100-metre sprint?
A. He had athlete's foot!

Q. Who is the school's shot put champion?
A. Eva Brick!

Q. What has eleven heads and runs around screaming?
A. A school hockey team!

Q. Why did the boy turn up to sports day with some barbed wire under his arm?
A. He thought he'd try his luck at fencing!

Q. What do long-distance runners do when they forget something?
A. They jog their memory!

Q. What has 22 legs and goes "crunch, crunch, crunch!"
A. The school football team eating crisps!

Q. Why do football players do well in school?
A. Because they use their heads!

Q. Did you hear about the school's slowest swimmer?
A. He could only do the crawl!

Q. Why did the teacher jump into the pool?
A. She wanted to test the water!

Tennis Tomfoolery

Q. What sport are waiters best at?
A. Tennis, because they can serve so well!

Q. What's tennis player's favourite city?
A. Volleywood!

Q. What can you serve but never eat?
A. A tennis ball!

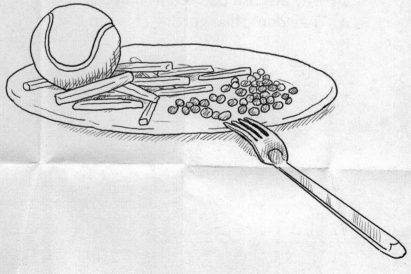

Knock, knock.
Who's there?
Tennis.
Tennis who?
Tennis is five plus five!

Q. Why are tennis players bad at relationships?
A. Nobody wants to have love!

Q. Why did the tennis player hold his shoe to his ear?
A. Because he liked sole music!

Q. Why are fish bad tennis players?
A. They don't like getting close to the net!

Q. Why did the tennis players all rush to the court?
A. Because first come, first serve!

Q. Where do zombies play tennis?
A. On a tennis corpse!

Q. Why did the elephant float down the river on his back?
A. So he wouldn't get his tennis shoes wet!

Q. What do you get if you cross a skunk and a pair of tennis rackets?
A. Ping pong!

Terrific Trampolining

Q. What music does a trampoline enjoy?
A. Hip Hop!

Q. Why did the dog refuse to take up trampolining?
A. Because he was a Boxer!

Q. What happened when the trampoline springs were tightened?
A. The trampolinist hit the roof!

Q. Why wasn't the trampolinist surprised when she won a gold medal?
A. She always knew she would reach great heights!

Q. Why do trampoline coaches enjoy their jobs?
A. Because of the ups and downs!

Q. What do trampolinists do when they get ill?
A. Hope they bounce back soon!

Q. What is the best time of year to take up trampolining?
A. Spring!

Wacky Weightlifting

Q. What bird is the best weightlifter?
A. The crane!

Q. Did you hear about the weightlifting vegetable?
A. He was a muscle sprout!

Q. Why did the weightlifter strap a dictionary to each arm?
A. He wanted his arms to have definition!

Q. What makes a weightlifter smile?
A. His facial muscles!

Witty Wrestling

Q. Why did the wrestler always carry a key?
A. To get out of hammerlocks!

Q. What do wrestler's drinks come in?
A. Six packs!

1st Wrestler: I hear you're taking a mail-order bodybuilding course?
2nd Wrestler: Yes. Every week the postman brings me a new piece of bodybuilding equipment.
1st Wrestler: You don't look any different though.
2nd Wrestler: I know, but you should see how muscular my postman is!

Smashing Sports Books

'RUNNING SLOWLY' BY ISA COMING

'Will He Win?' by Betty Wont

'COPING WITH LOSING AT SPORTS' BY ANNE GUSH

'He Must Win' by Elsie Cries

'KNOCKED OUT' BY ESAU STARS

'World's Greatest Wrestlers' by Everhard Muscles

'KUNG FU WITH YOUR CHUMS' BY FLORA FRIEND

'Feeling Like a Winner' by U. Dunnit

'The Worst Striker' by Mr Goal

'PENALTY SHOOT-OUTS' BY HUGO FIRST

'My Greatest Goals' by Annette Buster

'How To Put Your Football Boots On' by Neil Down

'KEEP ON TRYING' BY PERCY VERE

'The Day After a Marathon' by A. King

'How I Win Races' by Aaron Quigley

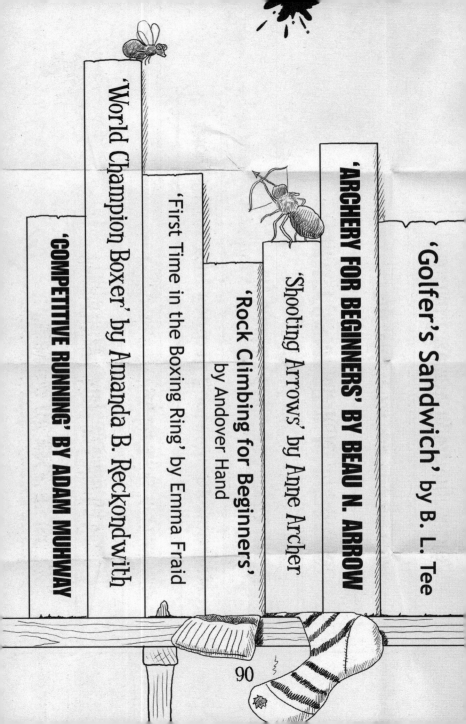

'World Champion Boxer' by Amanda B. Reckondwith

'First Time in the Boxing Ring' by Emma Fraid

'Rock Climbing for Beginners' by Andover Hand

'Shooting Arrows' by Anne Archer

'**ARCHERY FOR BEGINNERS' BY BEAU N. ARROW**

'Golfer's Sandwich' by B. L. Tee

'**COMPETITIVE RUNNING' BY ADAM MUHWAY**

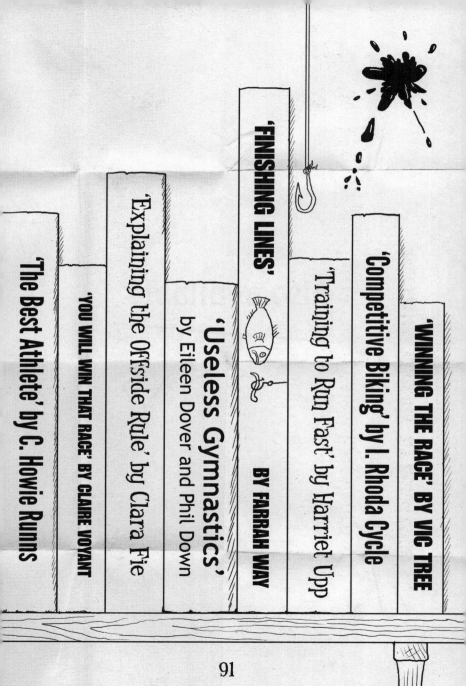

'WINNING THE RACE' BY VIC TREE

'Competitive Biking' by I. Rhoda Cycle

'Training to Run Fast' by Harriet Upp

'FINISHING LINES'

'Useless Gymnastics'
by Eileen Dover and Phil Down

BY FARRAH WAY

'Explaining the Offside Rule' by Clara Fie

'YOU WILL WIN THAT RACE' BY CLAIRE VOYANT

'The Best Athlete' by C. Howie Runns

Also available

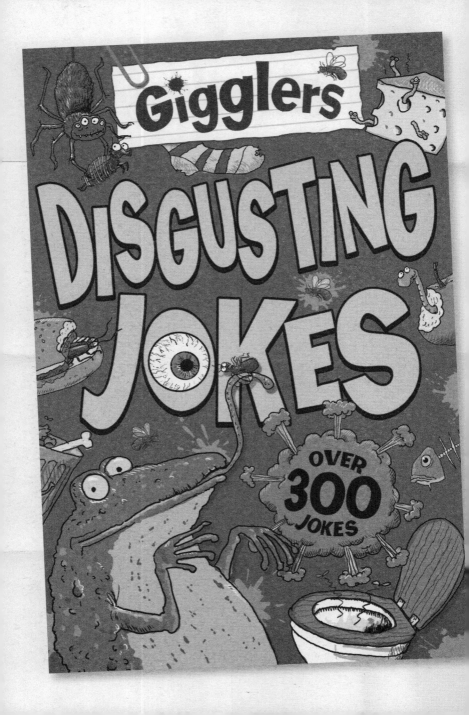

Coming soon
BEASTLY JOKES